D1207008

EARTH'S TREASURES
TURQUOISE

CHRISTINE PETERSEN
ABDO Publishing Company

visit us at
www.abdopublishing.com

Published by ABDO Publishing Company, PO Box 398166, Minneapolis, MN 55439.
Copyright © 2014 by Abdo Consulting Group, Inc. International copyrights reserved in all
countries. No part of this book may be reproduced in any form without written permission from
the publisher. The Checkerboard Library™ is a trademark and logo of ABDO Publishing Company.

Printed in the United States of America, North Mankato, Minnesota.
052013
012014

 PRINTED ON RECYCLED PAPER

Cover Photo: iStockphoto
Interior Photos: Alamy pp. 5, 7, 11, 13, 20, 21, 29; AP Images pp. 19. 24; Corbis pp. 9, 16, 17, 23;
    Getty Images pp. 4, 22, 26; iStockphoto pp. 1, 10–11, 15–16, 18, 27

Editors: Rochelle Baltzer, Tamara L. Britton
Art Direction: Neil Klinepier

Library of Congress Control Number: 2013932671

Cataloging-in-Publication Data

Petersen, Christine.
 Turquoise / Christine Petersen.
   p. cm. -- (Earth's treasures)
ISBN 978-1-61783-875-0
Includes bibliographical references and index.
1. Turquoise--Juvenile literature. 2. Mineralogy--Juvenile literature. I. Title.
553.8--dc23

                                      2013932671

CONTENTS

Enduring Treasure

In 1899, British **archaeologist** Sir William Matthew Flinders Petrie arrived in the Egyptian city of Abydos. Five thousand years ago, Abydos was home to Egypt's first kings and queens. It was also the site of a large **necropolis**.

Sir Flinders Petrie

Abydos was now just a ruin. Grave robbers had broken into its tombs and temples in search of treasure. An earlier research team had behaved almost as badly. They took anything that seemed valuable. They destroyed almost everything else. Petrie hoped something remained that would help tell the story of these ancient people.

Djer was the third king in Egypt's first dynasty. Petrie's team carefully opened his tomb. The rooms and their contents were wrecked. Petrie peeked into a hole in a wall.

Inside were the broken bones of a human arm. Bracelets dangled from the wrist. One of them was made of gold. Gold and turquoise plaques dangled from it. Each was crowned by a falcon. Petrie had discovered something remarkable. It was the oldest royal jewelry ever found.

This is King Djer's tomb at Abydos. Egypt's early kings were not buried in pyramids.

MIGHTY MINERAL

Throughout history, people have made items to be worn for decoration. Early jewelry was made of shells, pebbles, clay, and bone.

Later, people made jewelry from minerals. One of the most precious was turquoise. Turquoise is a blue-green mineral that forms near Earth's surface.

Several thousand minerals occur on Earth. Each is **unique**. Yet, they all share certain properties. Minerals are typically solid rather than liquid or gaseous. And, they are **inorganic**.

Minerals are composed of chemical elements. The smallest part of an element is an atom. Some minerals contain atoms of only one element. For example, diamond is made of only carbon atoms. Turquoise contains five or more elements.

In every mineral, the atoms link together in a specific pattern. The linked atoms form a solid, three-dimensional crystal. Turquoise crystals may gather into round nuggets that look like clusters of grapes. Others form long, narrow veins that course through rock.

Turquoise's key elements are aluminum, copper, hydrogen, oxygen, and phosphorus.

EARTH'S GIFT

Earth's crust is like that of a pie. Cut through it and you will reach another layer that is completely different! Beneath the crust is the mantle. It is made of hot, liquid rock called **magma**.

Volcanic eruptions can send bubbles or jets of magma up into the crust. There, it slowly cools, forming layers of igneous rock.

Thick layers of rock press down on each other within the crust. This pressure creates heat. Water is found in many of these layers. The heated water trickles along, slowly breaking down the

EARTH'S LAYERS

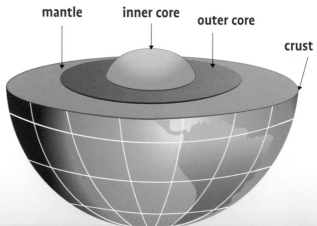

mantle   inner core   outer core   crust

8

surrounding rock. In this way, atoms of copper, phosphorus, and aluminum are released.

This syrupy solution of water and elements oozes into the rock. It fills cracks and air pockets. As it cools, turquoise is formed.

The shape of a turquoise deposit depends on the space in which it forms.

WORKS OF ART

Each turquoise deposit is a natural work of art. Stones from one mine may look entirely different from those in another. These differences are caused by impurities.

A variety of elements may be present as turquoise is forming. Pure turquoise is as blue as the sky on a warm summer's day. This color comes from a particular balance of copper and aluminum in the mineral.

However, iron can sometimes replace aluminum atoms in the crystal structure. When this happens, the mineral has a green shade. Greater amounts of iron deepen the green color. Zinc atoms cause turquoise to look yellow.

Impurities can affect other qualities of the stone. Aluminum is a soft metal element, while zinc is hard. Turquoise containing zinc tends to be

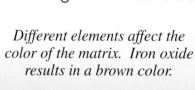

Different elements affect the color of the matrix. Iron oxide results in a brown color.

more durable. It does not crack or crumble as easily. However, many jewelry buyers prefer bright blue turquoise to the yellow stones.

Some turquoise has dark veins running through it. Experts call this a matrix. This is partially melted rock that poured into the spaces within a cooling turquoise deposit.

Pure turquoise has no matrix.

THE SOURCE

Turquoise was among the first gemstones mined from the earth. In King Djer's time, it was mined in the Sinai Peninsula. Ancient Egyptians described the area as "the terraces of turquoise."

Sinai is located far to the northeast of Abydos. It lies within modern Egypt's borders. But, it was not part of Djer's territory. Still, Egyptians established mines there. They mined turquoise until 1069 BCE.

Turquoise was also mined in ancient Persia, or present-day Iran. It was collected in the Asian countries of China and Tibet. The South American nation of Peru also produced turquoise for many years.

Today, the United States is the most important source of turquoise. There are active mines in Arizona, Nevada, California, Colorado, and New Mexico. Smaller amounts of the mineral are mined in China, Australia, Tibet, South America, Europe, and western Asia.

Today, remains of Egyptian mines can still be seen on the Sinai Peninsula.

North
America

South
America

Top Turquoise-Producing Countries

- 🪓 Australia
- 🪓 China
- 🪓 Egypt
- 🪓 Iran
- 🪓 Tibet
- 🪓 United States

Europe

Asia

Africa

Australia

N
W E
S

TRADING TURQUOISE

In North America, native people discovered their own turquoise source in present-day New Mexico. They called it Chalchihuitl. The name came from an Aztec word meaning "green stone."

In the desert near Mount Chalchihuitl was a great city called Chaco. Native peoples from Chaco used stone axes, picks, and hammers to remove turquoise from the mountainside.

Turquoise became an important part of religious rituals. So, other people wanted to get some. Tribes from Mexico offered to trade colorful parrot feathers for turquoise. They also sent copper bells and seashells. Turquoise from Mount Chalchihuitl has been discovered throughout North America.

Turquoise from Mount Chalchihuitl has been found inlaid in Aztec artifacts.

16

Today, people may visit Chaco at Chaco Culture National Historic Park.

In Chaco, lapidaries were specially trained to carve turquoise and other minerals. Their art was a slow process. It required time and patience.

To begin, the freshly mined turquoise was washed to remove dirt and loose grit. The stone was rubbed repeatedly against a flat block of rough sandstone. Bit by bit, its rough edges were smoothed and polished.

The artist drilled holes in the turquoise with a sharpened piece of chert. This created beads and pendants. **Fetishes** were carved in the shape of familiar animals.

Inlay was another important art form. Small, flat pieces of turquoise were chipped from a larger block. These were fitted together on jewelry or larger surfaces. Hundreds of pieces of inlay were sometimes arranged to form a **mosaic** picture or design.

A Perfect Pair

Navajo, Zuñi, Pueblo, and Hopi Native Americans are related to the ancient people of Chaco. Members of these tribes are some of the world's best lapidaries and jewelry designers.

In the mid-1800s, Hispanic settlers to the Southwest taught Navajo people how to work with silver. Navajo **silversmiths** passed the skill along to Zuñi neighbors. In turn, the Zuñi showed Hopi people how to make jewelry from silver.

A silver ring with two turquoise cabochons

18

Silver and turquoise make a perfect pair. When heated, silver is easily bent and twisted into many shapes. Delicate designs can be cut onto its surface.

To make jewelry, turquoise was often cut into **cabochons**. These were then fixed in place with a bezel, or narrow rim, of silver.

A Zuñi lapidary

19

Squash blossom necklaces

A favorite Native American jewelry design is the squash blossom necklace. The pendant is shaped like an upside-down U. It may be **etched** or fitted with **cabochons**.

Turquoise stones line both sides of the chain. Their silver settings look like the tube-shaped flowers of a squash plant. This pattern represents growth and the blessings of life.

A Pueblo Native American models his squash blossom necklace.

21

TALISMAN

In 1912, the National Association of Jewelers created an official list of birthstones. A gemstone was chosen to represent each month of the year.

Birthstones are meant to be **talismans**. Over time, the list of birthstones has expanded. Today, turquoise is one of the birthstones for December.

Many people believe that turquoise brings wisdom, creativity, and kindness to its wearer. Historically, turquoise was used as

Since the Middle Ages, a gift of turquoise and ruby jewelry has been a pledge of love.

Find Your Birthstone!

January — garnet

February — amethyst

March — aquamarine

April — diamond

May — emerald

June — pearl

protection against evil spirits. Those who rode horseback also made sure to own a piece of turquoise. The stone was supposed to protect against falls.

During the **Middle Ages**, turquoise was a symbol of friendship or love. That tradition continued for many centuries. In 1840, Britain's Queen Victoria married Germany's Prince Albert. The couple designed a special gift for her **bridesmaids**. Each received a silver brooch shaped like an eagle. The eagle's body was covered with tiny round turquoise stones of the purest blue.

To ancient Egyptians, green feldspar (above) *and turquoise represented new life.*

| July | August | September | October | November | December |
| ruby | peridot | sapphire | opal | topaz | turquoise |

23

A Stronger Stone

Strong samples of natural turquoise are rare. Most turquoise is stabilized before it is made into jewelry.

There is another popular myth about turquoise. It is said to change color when the owner is sick or when danger is near. It returns to its normal color when all is well. This may seem like magic. It is actually a weakness of the mineral.

Turquoise is **porous**. A person who is frightened or ill may perspire. Sweat can be drawn into the stone, darkening its color. Other liquids, oils, and chemicals have the same effect.

Because of this quality, most turquoise is not very strong. It rates between 5 and 6 on the Mohs Hardness Scale. It may crumble when mined or carved. And, it can crack or shatter if dropped.

MOHS HARDNESS SCALE

MOHS HARDNESS	MINERAL	HARDNESS OF OTHER MATERIALS
1	talc	
2	gypsum	2.2 fingernail
3	calcite	3.2 copper penny
4	fluorite	
5	apatite	5.1 pocketknife
6	orthoclase	6.5 steel needle
7	quartz	7.0 streak plate
8	topaz	
9	corundum	
10	diamond	

(SOFTEST ↓ HARDEST)

This weakness has been a problem for thousands of years. Ancient lapidaries soaked the stone in animal fat. Oil seeped into the pores, filling the air spaces.

Today, most turquoise is stabilized. To do this, the stone is heated to remove any water trapped inside. Clear liquid plastic called resin is injected into it. Dyes can be added to darken its color. After the plastic dries, the stone is stronger and shinier. It can be polished and carved like natural turquoise.

Is It Turquoise?

Turquoise can be quite expensive. But, there are other options if you want the look of turquoise without its high price.

Reconstituted turquoise is made from bits and pieces too small for any other use. These are crumbled to a powder and mixed with resin. The mixture is poured into a pan. After drying, the material is cut into sections. Then it can be carved and polished like other forms of turquoise.

Imitation turquoise is also available. Certain minerals can be dyed to look like turquoise. But, they have

Steatite is also called soapstone.

One of these gems is howlite and the other one is turquoise. Can you tell which is which?

an entirely different chemical structure.

Steatite was used in ancient Egypt when turquoise was not available. Howlite is a white mineral. It has veins that look like matrix. Dyed blue, it passes for turquoise in modern jewelry. Block turquoise is made from plastic.

The blue stone is howlite. The green stone is turquoise.

START A COLLECTION

There are many ways to start your own turquoise collection. You can be a miner for a day at Royston Mines near Tonopah, Nevada. Visitors are not allowed inside the mine. However, you can mine turquoise from a pile of **tailings**.

If mining does not interest you, try a gem and mineral show. The Tucson Gem and Mineral Show is the largest in the United States. It is held in Tucson, Arizona, the second full weekend in February.

Become a Rock Hound!

WOULD YOU LIKE TO START YOUR OWN COLLECTION OF GEMS AND MINERALS? BECOME A ROCK HOUND!

To get started, locate a site likely to have the treasures you seek. Before you head out, be sure it is legal and you have permission to collect specimens from your search area. Then, gather the tools and safety gear you'll need. Don't forget to bring an adult!

Label your treasures with the date and location you found them. Many rock hounds set a goal for their collections. For example, they might gather samples of all the minerals found in their state or province.

Finally, always leave the land in better shape than you found it. Respecting the environment helps preserve it for future rock hounds and the rest of your community.

WHAT WILL YOU NEED?
map
compass
magnifying glass
hard hat or bicycle helmet
safety goggles
sunscreen
bucket
shovel
rock hammer
pan or screen box
containers for your finds

An artist selects turquoise at the Tucson Gem and Mineral Show.

There, you can find mineral, gem, fossil, lapidary, and jewelry **exhibits**. Arizona is a top turquoise-producing state. There should be many fine examples to choose from!

If you want to stay near home, visit your local gem and mineral shop. But beware! You may spend hours gazing at the marvelous minerals on display. Isn't it amazing that such a treasure is hidden inside the earth? It is a good reminder that beauty is all around us.

GLOSSARY

archaeologist (ahr-kee-AH-luh-jihst) - one who studies the remains of people and activities from ancient times.

bridesmaid - a woman who is an attendant of the bride during a wedding.

cabochon - a gem or a bead that is carved so that it is curved or rounded outward, like a dome.

etch - to make a pattern or design on a hard surface with a substance that eats into the surface, such as acid.

exhibit - to make something available for people to see.

fetish - an object that is believed to have magical powers.

inorganic - being or made of matter other than plant or animal.

magma - melted rock beneath Earth's surface.

Middle Ages - a period in European history that lasted from about 500 CE to about 1500 CE.

mosaic - decoration made from small pieces of glass, stone, or wood. Different-colored pieces are fitted together to create a design.

necropolis (nuh-KRAH-puh-luhs) - a large, fancy cemetery in an ancient city.

porous - having small holes that allow air or liquids to pass through.

reconstitute - to return something to a former state by adding a liquid.

silversmith - an artisan who makes things out of silver.

tailings - refuse produced from processing ore.

talisman - an object that is believed to have magic powers.

unique - being the only one of its kind.

SAYING IT

Abydos - uh-BYE-duhs

Chalchihuitl - chahl-chee-WHEE-tuhl

Djer - DEE-juhr

igneous - IHG-nee-uhs

lapidary - LA-puh-dehr-ee

Zuñi - ZOO-nee

WEB SITES

To learn more about turquoise, visit ABDO Publishing Company online. Web sites about turquoise are featured on our Book Links page. These links are routinely monitored and updated to provide the most current information available.

www.abdopublishing.com

INDEX